HOW TO BUILD WEALTH FROM SCRATCH

A Father's Guide To His Child On Early Retirement

E.I. KELVIN

Copyright © 2017 by E.I. Kelvin

All rights reserved. No part of this publication may be reproduced, stored in a retrieval system, or transmitted in any form or by any means – electronics, mechanical, photocopying, recording, or otherwise – without the written permission of the publisher.

For more information, please contact

kelsdadevin@gmail.com

ISBN – 13: 978-1546617211
ISBN – 10: 1546617213

Contents

INTRODUCTION

Chapter One
  Image Effect

Chapter Two
  Sacrificial Years

Chapter Three
  Investment Period

Chapter Four
  Early Retirement Phase

Chapter Five
  On Love and Family

Chapter Six
  Health

Chapter Seven
  Maintaining Wealth

Chapter Eight
  Legacy

INTRODUCTION

Dear Child,

I know you will be wondering why I am dedicating this book to you when we have not spoken for a while now, just do us a favor and read until the very end.

You are now at the crossroad of life, where decisions you make henceforth will have a huge impact on how you live the productive and non-productive part of your life, I will beg you to understand every sentence, and be wisely flexible in executing them. I said "Flexible" because my time may be different from yours, and if you wish to give this to your child, his time may be different from ours.

Imbedded in this book are principles, way of life, morals - call it whatever you deem fit, but they will aid you in being a better gentleman than I am and your empire won't be a tall dream. I will be as real as it gets, that is to say, I will not sugarcoat anything.

Herein, I will be talking about Wealth, Love, Family, Legacy and Health, mind you, all are pillars of greatness and do not take any for granted, regardless of what you think is currently important, because all pillars are important.

If you feel I have no right to give you advice on life issues, I sincerely apologize for the notion I have embedded in your heart over the years, for the purpose of this book, do not see me as a father, but see me as a Gentleman who has come to guide you through the journey of life.

Chapter One

Image Effect

I am glad you have chosen this path, but I want you to forget everything you know about life, I want you to forget everything society told you is the norm, I want your mind to be as blank as fresh slate yet eager for knowledge as a zealous pupil does. To begin with, I want you to know and believe that the world we live in is a stage and nothing lasts forever. We all come and go, so how do we make our time worthwhile?

Think of a child and think of these things: When you came to this world, were your born with anyone around you today? When you spoke your first words, did you say what people expected you to say? When you began taking your first steps, were you not restricted out of "love", yet your stubbornness made walking quicker? When you began having dreams, were they not clear and achievable without validation? When you slept as a child, was there a fear of what tomorrow will bring? However, as we grow older, due to societal influence, we forget who we are and the basis of how we do the simple things. Soon, all that is going to change with you as you begin to see more light to the essence of living.

In my early years in high school, there were tales of the legendary ball juggler who was nicknamed Jobinho, every soccer player in school wanted to be like him. People said he was given the ball to juggle by the coach as punishment, insisting that once the ball touches the ground he would do fifty push-ups and continue until he was satisfied. But Jobinho with his actions humiliated the coach by juggling the ball for three hours without it touching the ground, in fact, it was another teacher who took the ball away from him as he juggled and told him to leave, leaving the students cheering. Jobinho was the best, and the thought of this alone made potential ball jugglers scared of him. He won all juggling competitions by a landslide, and as time went on, he intimidated anyone he wished to humiliate because he had the talent and fame. On a fateful Sunday, a junior from nowhere relegated him to nothing, the godlike Jobinho was reduced to a mere man, and he was defeated in the worst way ever – in a juggling competition that he organized. The cheer shifted to the new hero and those who once held almighty Jobinho in high regards chanted songs of praise around the school. From then on, he disappeared into the shadows; and little heard of him again, giving room to the new kid on the block to reign.

You may be wondering why I shared this weird story, but I want you to understand the facts, even if I may not be a good storyteller, and know that this is not a storybook. Later on, I knew why the great Jobinho in the latter days fell from grace, and how an unknown Bob became champion.

The coach Jobinho humiliated never forgave him for it (as I would like to put it, even if he insisted there was no hard feelings), and so he picked interest in Bob - the junior that turned out to be the new champion. He trained him on juggling (mind you he already showed glimpses of being a good juggler, that was why he was recruited by the coach), as Jobinho washed himself with the praises and cheers of the crowd. Bob's interview stated that he had intensive training with his coach for six months, and on the seventh month, he became champion. The stage of Bob's training that struck me later on in life was not the normal ball juggling training, but the one-month "intensive physiological exercise" that was the seed to the tree he became. I was fortunate to meet the coach later on in life, and we had drinks at the pub, I reminded him of the Bob and Jobinho story, and how he played a crucial role in training Bob to be the best, he simply said;

"When I met Bob, he was a shy kid that saw himself as average; he even got bullied a lot. However, watching him juggle when he was happy I saw talent, talent he even could not see. So I decided to him develop the talent, and I told him I will coach him for a while until he was ready, I also made him promise not to participate in any juggling competition for that period until I asked him to. He was happy, he did not even want to participate because he thought less of himself, and I felt that was a problem. Therefore, the first month, the only thing he did was look in the mirror and say, "I am the best at what I do, people look at me and see a cat, but I look at me and see a cub that is going to be a lion, not just any lion, but a great lion". He said that for one month before we started the real training, and I was not surprised before and after training, he would go to the mirror and repeat those words over and over again. I didn't even know bullies called him Bobcat because he was a little chubby, and Jobinho called him Bobcat on the day of the competition and he replied by saying he was silly not to know the difference between a cat, a lion, and a great lion. That's how he won, he believed in himself first.

The first thing I want you to work on is yourself; by this, I mean how you view yourself. It doesn't matter if you are ugly or handsome, it doesn't matter if you are qualified or not, it doesn't matter how much you currently have in the bank, what matters is what you believe about you. The mind has a funny way of either elevating or demoting without you even taking any action and it all begins with what you have fed it prior to the event. For the next month, you will be working on your mindset and how you want people to view you. Constantly look in the mirror and tell yourself how awesome you are, and how great you would become. It sounds petty and even unnecessary, but believe me; for progress to be achieved, self-image must be worked on. There is a popular fable about an eaglet that was unfortunate as an egg to be taken from her nest by a farmer and put together with hen's egg. Once she hatched, she was taught the ways of a chicken – she scratched the surface of the ground looking for worms to eat. She would look above her, see birds flying, and always wonder why she never flew. One day, while searching for worms close to the river, she saw an image of herself and from then on the mindset she had changed. "I cannot be scratching the ground looking for worms and always running in search of a hideout when the hulk disturbs" Saying that, she flapped her wings and discovered she could fly, and she did fly to the very end of the sky never to return to the life of scratching the ground for worms.

You are what you believe, so my child, I want you to know and believe in the fact that you are great and one of a kind. Believe in that positive image of yourself and say it to the mirror before you leave the house for the next one-month. Mind you, it is not just to say it, as you interact with people, have it ring in your head how great you are and how you cannot settle for less. Do not read further until you have this belief resonate on your attitude towards life and how you interact with people. A great person knows he is great and works until he achieves that greatness, I will warn you again that this is not going to be a day's job, but will require constant discipline, commitment and a certain level of sacrifice. Are you a lion king in the jungle, or a sheep among the flocks in the stable? Are you an eagle with liberty to soar in the sky or are you a chicken limited to scratching the ground for worms? For the next month dear child, I want you to constantly look into the mirror and tell yourself who you are and who you want to become, believing in every word you utter.

Chapter Two

Sacrificial Years

Now that you know, who you are and who you want to become, this stage is usually the hardest part, and you might find my methods primitive or unnecessary to achieve that pinnacle you want to achieve. Imagine you are faced with a mountain, for the past month, you have come to understand who you are and who you want to become, but for you to be that person, you need to get yourself to the top of that mountain or continue living the life you now see reason to leave. For you to climb this mountain, you must have certain tools that will not be found in the tool shop.

- Sacrifice
- Diligence
- Knowledge
- Discipline

- Luck

Interestingly, since all the above cannot be bought in the tool shop, they must be learnt and constantly practiced. The next five-year-period (Or whatever number of years you shall decide to realistically set for yourself) we shall call the "sacrificial period", because it will be a period where you will have to deprive yourself of many things. This can only be achieved through Discipline, Due Diligence in the craft of obtaining the required Knowledge and awaiting the period the world will call Luck.

As I have stated, it all begins with the mind; the willingness to make the decision to climb the mountain is a major key to reaching the top. Likewise, your mind must believe in this sacrificial period and make your body carry out all that is needed to make it a reality. For the sake of the reality on ground in my time, I will put forth this period to be five years, so for the next five years, you will be working with the tools stated above in achieving a set goal.

Right after school, I was fortunate enough to gain employment into a reputable bank, and as you would expect, the pay was mouthwatering. Prior to that, I couldn't afford many things so, as my salary came, I bought all I believed I needed and wanted. Friday was the best part of my week, I and many other colleagues would visit the best clubs in town and spend lots of money having fun. We took pride in showing off the latest toy or gadget. This was a routine for us, for we derived joy in painting the city black. However, another colleague of ours rarely followed us out for parties or came for occasions. Mind you, he wasn't anti-social, because whenever he attended he was the life of the party. Everyone loved him, and wanted him to be present for his/her occasion, but he was always polite in turning down invitations. Rumors began to spread that he had family issues to take care of, and that was the reason he was not always present for events. This made people pity him and love him the more. After five years of a lovely time in the banking sector, our nation was in a recession, and many of us became jobless. You might be thinking it would not affect us since we were bankers and knew the profitable investments to indulge in, but you would be wrong. It is true that we had access to information about investments and had easy credit access, but we spent so much money and time socializing and increasing our social status that very few of us thought about the period where there will be nothing. Stocks were at an all-time low, companies were retrenching at an unprecedented rate, unemployment was at its peak, inflation was rising, the government itself was confused, and citizens were suffering because they did not plan for this.

During this period, I was depressed, bills were piling up, I even sold my Rolex to feed for a period, and it wasn't an easy ride. Few years down the line, I had an interview with a company for an accounting role, and was shocked when the CEO gave me a call and said "It's been a while old friend, but I don't think the role suits you, a chief accountant is more like it, what do you say?" I was stunned, that colleague of ours that rarely showed up for occasions was the CEO and just offered me a job. I had tears in my eyes after our conversation because I was saying to myself "How is it that you lost so much these few years, and your colleague progressed without a sweat". I worked for him for a long period, but it took me a long time to grasp the method of his success, and I will share this with you as we progress.

Do you remember when I stated that for five years we painted the city black in the early stage of our career? Well, during that period he had other plans. He confessed to me that he had no family issue, and was surprised when it became news, he just did not deny or accept it, but used it to his advantage. He said he had a goal to save certain percentage of his salary and other benefits, and so did not have the luxury of constantly frequenting occasions. He admitted to always envying us, but he had a set goal and he believed it was more important than constant socializing. My friend got the same salary as everyone for that period, but before an eight-year period, he had his company. He was simply frugal in spending, and kept his eyes on what he wanted, the recession only gave him more courage to do what he has always wanted – to be his own boss. While we were living for the moment, he was carefully planning his empire, and he had his own share of fun despite this. I learnt a lot from him over time, and I must admit I should have done better with the knowledge I got.

Now you are done with school, I don't care how good or bad your grades are, I don't even care if you chose to drop out, just see it as an advantage to climbing to the mountain peak. Be mindful of the crowd, they are inexperienced in the area of getting wealth. Be wary of those that seek quick wealth, it's like vulgar seduction, it might not happen, and even if it does, it may not stand the test of time. I want you to understand the tools needed in this stage of your life; first, I want you to get a job!

If I had wealth like my colleague, maybe I would have given you a reasonable fraction to build an empire with, but I'll give you what I can and hope this knowledge is used properly. I beg that you get a job, regardless of your qualification. If you are fortunate to get a good paying job, good for you, and if not continue to try, volunteer to be an assistant to someone with work experience or better still, try to gain good work experience until you are blessed with one that pays. Wealth isn't built in a day, it takes time and a process, therefore do not feel the weight of the world when life doesn't smile at you as you give your best, but keep trying.

If you have secured a steady income stream for yourself that also gives you the ability to increase in knowledge due to experience, do not act like the crowd. Go for only important occasions to keep your face relevant, do not buy what you do not need, for a time will come when you will buy whatever you want, save as much as you can and don't stop saving. My colleague had a saving percentage of 50% of his income, analyze what works for you and stick to it, in all, always have it clearly written at the back of your mind that your employer cannot make you wealthy.

Sacrifice: Can you remember when I stated you get a job, or any kind of steady income? Well, that will make it easier for you not to borrow or seek favors that will be detrimental to you in the long run. A certain percentage of this income should be saved, as this would be used as capital when the time is right. That large house your colleagues are moving into wouldn't be required of you at this stage, that car that is expensive to maintain but makes a statement is also not necessary. That event that would require you to spend unreasonably should be avoided as often as possible, that vacation that wouldn't add any value to you asides pleasure should not be brought up in your dealings.

In all, those things that you pay a premium on which adds little or no value should be avoided. The best way is to have a mindset that allows you to despise such things and see them as unnecessary or a rip-off. It will not be easy, when you walk into a car dealer shop and you choose economy over luxury or when you hear stories of how your colleagues enjoyed the weekend or vacation. I know it won't be easy when you remember you have some amount of money saved up somewhere that's yielding little interest when you can please your desires with it, but it is called sacrifice. Sacrifice which I define simply as depriving yourself of an initial desire or need to enjoy a future benefit of your actions.

My colleague had to deal with the pain of sacrifice. However, what is gain without pain? It would not be appreciated. Likewise, this period won't be easy, but when you feel the urge to go against this principle, remember that the end is what matters most and not the beginning. Pleasure is addictive; therefore, I'll say to you that you must indulge less in it. Of all the pleasure that men indulge in, never fall into the trap of the pleasure of a *woman's lap*. Drink as little as you can, avoid smoking or doing any hard drugs, shun unnecessary eating habit, detest the premium lifestyle, and most of all, avoid unprofitable commitment to women, for they can blur your vision on the end goal of what you desire. Moderation is crucial in understanding the tool of sacrifice, never buy more than you need and never mix desires with needs.

The beautiful thing about sacrifice is the joy derived from its gain will always overshadow the initial pain, so you would not regret your actions at the end. Mind you, I have asked you initially to be flexible in your actions with the reality of your time, so make sure after you have saved that 50% (Or whatever is realistic to you) you make provisions for you to enjoy yourself in the best way possible. Socialize as often as you can, make friends, especially those in a different field from yours. Do not let fun elude you, life should be enjoyed. Sacrifice and do what is necessary.

Looking back, it is no coincidence my wealthy colleague only partied once a month, and when he did, he did it with more vigor than us.

In addition, you will not only be sacrificing your income and desires; you will also be sacrificing your time. After work hours, make sure weekends are not spent sleeping or relaxing; rather I will explain more on seeking knowledge when we talk more on that tool. I remember the story of a little girl who was always given biscuits (Which were her favorite) by her parents every time she went to school. Before entering school, she would divide it into equal half and give one-half to a beggar close to the school. She loved this biscuit so much, but chose to sacrifice her half, just so she can see a smile on the beggar's face when she dropped it for him to eat. One day on her way back home from school, she got hit by a truck and was rushed to the nearest hospital. She had lost a lot of blood, and needed blood for an operation, but her blood type was rare, and her parents were on vacation. Calls were placed to blood banks around by the hospital to no avail, the poor girl was dying, and no one present had a matching blood type. However, this beggar ran after the ambulance that brought her to the hospital, his friend that brought him biscuit so often was dying before his very eyes. He asked the nurse if they could check his blood to determine a match, after much hesitation, the test was positive. A call was placed to her panicking parents for approval, and you bet they did. A beggar, because of the sacrifices she made so often saved the little girl that day. It may sound like a story of chance, but imagine the beggar did not run all the way to the hospital and no blood bank could supply at the right time, she would have died.

Sacrificing won't be easy my child, but like I said this is going to be the difficult period. Whereas for the majority of your friends and colleagues it will be their best because they have little or no responsibility and plenty of income to spend. You are not like them; for you desire to build wealth, and there are prices you have to pay, so do not be discouraged, the earlier you decide to learn this, the better.

Diligence: You have a job, or a steady source of income that you save 50% of for a stipulated period (my take, five years), never let the pride of you having saved up more than your peers get to you. Diligence is being careful with the effort you put towards an objective in the long term. By this, I mean in your place of work, be efficient, be effective, be important, be the go-to person, and always seek to improve. Always be punctual to work, always arrive fifteen minutes to the meeting, never exceed your lunch period due to unnecessary preferences, and make sure you give your best in all you do. My colleague would say, work for the company like it is yours, and you will do things out of passion that will lead to steady improvement.

You know what you want to achieve, put it at the door of the office every morning and always focus on your task. Look for better ways to improve productivity, so you get more challenging tasks, and seek to increase productivity thereon. Always try to deliver way ahead of deadline, and you will have time to do other things. People will complain about workloads and so little time to do them, but diligence will make you self-conscious and a better manager of your time.

Your colleagues may see you as a workaholic, or a competitive person, because it will bring you favors with your managers or superior, but do not let it get to you, always be friendly to them to avoid unnecessary office politics. Due to diligence, you might be promoted or rewarded often, but remember to save more and do not let it change your personality or your attitude towards work and colleagues. Act humble; do not complain about the work, because your time there is limited. Learn as much as you can about your company and the industry or niche they operate, learn their strength, their weakness, learn how best it can improve, you will be amazed at how much you will develop in this short period.

As humble and diligent as you are, always network with people both within and outside your niche. Whenever you do not know, never feel too big to seek help, and always give credit as often as possible. During this period, some might want to take advantage of you, so learn how to say no when necessary, but be polite about it. You may also feel that you have an arsenal of savings and can loan colleagues, be wary of this, never borrow people what you cannot afford to forget, even if it's your boss. It's not a crime to say you do not have if it's above what you can afford to forget if things go south, and believe me this is very important.

As diligent as you may be, try to avoid office politics as much as you can, it's not healthy and the aftermath can be very toxic. See people around you as professionals, you just might need their help in future, so always avoid being in people's bad book, even the janitor, respect everyone. In addition, diligence can make people feel they owe you a favor or a reward, that's why I stated earlier that you could be promoted so often, but try not to owe favors. Learn to be independent, but not proud in seeking help when you need it, yet try as much as possible not to owe people favors, so they don't come back and ask that you do what you normally wouldn't want to do.

Every business's aim is to maximize profit, meaning numbers always speaks more volume in a capitalist system, so never forget that as diligently as you work. Treat your place of work like you own it, and you will avoid unnecessary waste and channel the savings to something that will yield more productivity. Have a good relationship with people around you, because you might need their help or recommendation in the long run.

In all your diligence, never forget to have time for yourself and things that are important to you, like friends and family. Do not be too overwhelmed with work that eating becomes a problem, or you forget a family function that would require your presence. There must be balance to work and life, always ensure you maintain that balance unapologetically.

Procrastination and laziness are the enemy of diligence, never give heed when their voices speak and your body begins to tingle, encourage yourself and stay focused on the end goal.

Knowledge: As diligent as you may be in your place of work, always keep your eyes and ears open to information. I have stated about the need to network and always being aware of your company, industry or niche's operations, this tool is crucial, as knowledge is power. Knowledge cannot be broadened without information, and you must learn how to filter information to your advantage.

As you network, learn, keep your ears open, and engage people in small talks that will be productive, know their strengths and weaknesses, understand human behavior, know the trends in the industry, and know about politics and how political decisions affect the economy. Learn basic knowledge Accounting, Economics, Finance, Marketing, and how it applies to both you and your niche. The ability to have the right information and the ability to use them at the right time makes you a knowledgeable person. Some people may have the same information you have, but may not know what to do with it, while others may have little information but utilize it in building an empire.

My wealthy colleague acquired so much knowledge in real estate, and during the recession, he used half of his savings to buy properties that he believed would be profitable in the long run, then he started a real-estate firm, and financed another firm that was into construction and had majority stake. He understood the market of the need for shelter and gathered knowledge in it during our time together in the bank. He would go for weekend seminars to broaden his horizon, he invested in himself by seeking knowledge in that niche that majority of the portfolio he handled during his time at the bank were real estate accounts. With this, his clientele base in the housing sector expanded so also did his knowledge that after during the recession, it wasn't difficult for him to blossom, because he was well equipped theoretically before he ventured into it.

Therefore, my child, when they say knowledge is power, believe them, but have it in mind that knowledge is more powerful when utilized properly. Invest in knowledge in whatever niche you feel is worth investing in; no knowledge is a waste, so broaden your horizon regardless. Talk to those excelling in whatever field you hold desire for, have a mentor in that field either directly or indirectly. Directly by being acquainted with them and having them share with you their principles, knowledge, belief, vision and even their hope. Indirectly by reading about them, reading the books they claim to have read, browsing through their lifestyle and their objective towards life, understanding their past and the actions they took, but most importantly learning from their success and mistakes.

Knowledge can be gotten from the most unlikely of places or people, so do not feel too big when seeking it. Information rules the world my child, gather as much as you can and utilize them practically, not just theoretically. The big difference with our educational system and life is that students are tested on what they know theoretically in our schools, but life will test you on how much knowledge you have and how best you can practically utilize this knowledge.

Please remember, do not go so extreme that you forget to live, seek knowledge diligently, and make yourself happy in the process. Always have your vision play out before engaging in anything. It's unwise for you to spend so much money in buying books you will end up not reading, or going for functions or seminars you will end up not listening, except the goal is to network. Always know what you want, and make sure what you do aligns with it, if it does not, spend your time on something more productive. Another beautiful thing about information is that it is easily gotten due to the advancement of modern technology; there are many channels to freely get them at little or no cost.

Do not hoard information, it's meant to be shared, share what you know with people, and they will willingly share what they know with you. That way you have enlightened someone, and gained more knowledge, free. No man is an island, do not act like you know it all or let pride have a place in your heart on your quest for knowledge.

Discipline: What makes a formidable army or team most of the time is their discipline. The ability to have a plan and follow it through takes discipline. You may know the importance of sacrifice (sweating it out today to enjoy tomorrow), being diligent, and obtaining knowledge, but to maintain this, one must master the tool of discipline. Discipline is having a controlled behavior, and bringing it into reality through your actions.

How my wealthy colleague could evade parties, drive one efficient car, live in a one room apartment that only had the necessaries, have the time to equip himself in knowledge, maintain his 50% saving rate, and still look good was simply due to discipline. He had a goal, and he made sure he saw it through. In his words "One must dream, but one must also work". We can dream all we want about how big we would be in future - just like when we were kids and we would brag about the number of cars we would have – but in order for this to become reality, we must work. Many people see wealthy people as those that are privileged, or those that used force labor to get what they want, but times have changed.

Discipline makes you avoid debt and owe unnecessary favors, because discipline helps you to be independent and know when best to seek people's help. Discipline helps avoid distractions, and constantly reminds you that there is a goal, regardless of the sound of the wind, you should carry on until you reach that goal. Discipline reminds you to shun unnecessary pursuit or friends that will be parasitic to your existence. Discipline will constantly remind you that there is time for everything, and as such refrain from pointless commitment and pleasure. Discipline blends all the tools together, making sure there is a balance in sacrifice, diligence and knowledge seeking. No matter what the crowd does or says, discipline makes you dead to their scorn, shows you the bigger picture, and strengthens your body to carry on in the quest to attain that goal.

The first task I stated was for you to look in the mirror for a month and tell yourself how great you are, and if you did this constantly, that means you have acquainted yourself with the ability to be disciplined. Distractions will surely come in different forms my child, but you must be determined enough to keep the balance with discipline. The world will call you names, friends will mock you, and women may avoid you because you do not do things they expect and are extremely frugal, the job may be stressful and demanding, events may occur that might leave you worried; but no pain, no gain.

On commitment, it might be a distraction, but if you are disciplined enough you will surely find a balance. Make sure whoever you have decided to commit with understands you as a person and what you want to achieve, if they share in your vision, they will stay, if not, better things lie ahead, and more will come. Do not tell the world you have a five-year savings somewhere, be disciplined enough to know when to talk and when to remain silent.

Keep to your schedule, have a plan and stick to it, manage your time well, know when to indulge in little talks, know when to network, know when to say no, know how to always be punctual, know the value of time; that is discipline. It easy to say, but harder to do, especially when you are used to living a lazy lifestyle, but with constant practice and motivating yourself with the end goal, it's not unattainable.

Luck: My wealthy colleague got into real estate when prices were down, people were looking for quick cash, and so housing prices came crashing. Companies needed liquid assets, and investors with cash were seen as messiahs. As the economy improved, those properties' value increased, companies' value also increased, and I told myself during the period I was working for him that he was just lucky. One day, he said to another wealthy man in my presence "The world will call it luck, but they will find it difficult to remember when you sacrificed, when you were disciplined, when you worked diligently, when you were seeking knowledge, and they will call your attainment of wealth; luck". It hit me so hard in the heart that I felt guilty, because even I myself tagged his attainment of wealth as luck.

Do not get me wrong, I am not saying some people are not lucky to be born into wealth, yet some people had a vision and made sure it became reality. You might not be fortunate to be born into a wealthy family, or stumble on wealth, but you can definitely build wealth from the scratch, there is no crime in that. However, we will call it what the world does, because they do not understand, we will call it luck. Do not frown at this and say luck is a thing of chance, but I tell you that with preparation, that chance will come and you will be ready to seize the moment, the world will then tag your fortune as luck, but you know deep down that you were preparing for it.

We have spoken about the tool called knowledge; it plays a crucial role in attainment of luck. As your mind, eyes and ears are open to information, and your savings have reached a substantial amount, a time will present itself before you when you will have to use that saving and invest in something that will be profitable in the end. By this, I do not mean any form of gambling; always run away from such, as they are addictive and often times would take from you more than you will end up benefitting from it.

You have amassed knowledge and network overtime, you know your strength and weakness, you know what niche you are willing to operate, you know how it operates, you have contacts of the right people, keep your options open, because you will find something worthwhile that will spark your interest. When this presents itself, strike. Take advantage of all the resources you have at your disposal, and utilize them effectively. They will say you are lucky when you decide to take this leap, but people call what they do not understand luck, and you understand perfectly well what you are doing.

Luck will birth the next period of your life, and I want you to remember that trees were once tiny seeds, but with constant supply of sunlight, water and the right soil, they grew into the tall giants they are today. A farmer knows this, knows what is required, and so always makes sure what the seed needs to become a tree is provided. Likewise you at this stage, you are that seed, and have nourished yourself constantly through the sacrifice, diligence, knowledge seeking and discipline, now opportunity is before you to become a tree, do not let it elude you.

This next period of your life, we shall call the Investment period. Investments are simply opportunities that were not neglected. As I have repetitively stated, people will call you lucky when your tree begins to bear fruit, but to you, you prepared for it. I have asked you to seek knowledge and build on it, because it is not advisable to invest in something you do not understand. During your sacrificial period, many opportunities will present themselves before you, but be patient and only strike when you have the required knowledge and you are certain it is right.

Dear child, remember my time may be different from yours, and so flexibility is advised. You may choose to invest your savings yearly in safe but profitable venture so they multiply other than seeking compounded interest from the bank on savings. In all, the goal is to amass the required capital that will get you started in building wealth without borrowing much but only when necessary. You might be unfortunate not to get a steady income channel in time, but do not worry, keep trying. In addition, you may have needs that might eat into your savings, do not give up, and try again. Finally, you may likely indulge in an opportunity that will end up not being profitable, you did not fail, you only gained more knowledge on what to do and what not to do, so try again. Surround yourself with people that will encourage and support you, no man is an island. Share your ideas, you can build a team or even have a partner from there. I commend you for attaining this stage of your life, do not lose focus now, and keep thinking big.

Chapter Three

Investment Period

"Take away the riches of a wealthy man, and in due time he will become wealthy again." My wealthy colleague said to me. That's because they understand the process it takes to attain wealth, and they are willing to go through it repeatedly. You will be disappointed on your way up, do not take disappointment to heart or it will bring you down. I'll share with you some of the advice I have gotten from him and other wealthy people overtime. These things are indeed no secret, somewhere in our subconscious we know that these processes should be followed, but the lust for living makes people act the way they do, that they do not put any of this to practice. Once you have saved or gotten enough, and you are indeed sure your knowledge is good, do not delay in investing. A simple motivation is that money begets money, that is you need money to make more money, and you are on the right track. During this period, you might have the notion of leaving your job, but my child, if you can operate your investments alongside your job, do not quit yet, as long as it breaks no law. When the time is right, you will know, as everything will fall in place. As you invest in your area of knowledge, never think of short-term gains, make sure your investment has a long-term mission.

There are many problems the world faces today, surprisingly it could be as minute as poor or slow service, focus on investments that solves these problems. The larger the people affected by these problems are, the more rewarding your business will be when you proffer solutions to them. From food, to clothing, to shelter, to transportation, to services, to technology, to health, whatever specialization you might pick interest in investing, always make sure they are solving a problem. This is business, there is no friend in business, so always ensure you do not let emotions becloud your reasoning, because situations of such will definitely present itself before you. Another thing you must have in mind is never to sell oranges still on the tree, it may be that it never ripens, or the wind blows them beyond sight. But pluck them, gather them, before you sell them, and then the heart can be at rest for tomorrow's sake.

A friend of ours Abraham invested in clothing long ago, he was so confident that the returns will be positive due to the high demand that he quit his job to focus on his investment. He took a loan from the bank that amounted to his expected profit and he started living a lavish lifestyle. Mind you, his investment was still at the maturity stage, and he wasn't putting much effort on gathering the right knowledge to reduce cost. He had a model, and wasn't flexible about improving it. Someone came along, and told him he could have more savings on cost and he should make him a partner, he was ready to pay the necessary price, but Abraham didn't listen, he thought they wanted to take his investment away from him, his way was his way. Not more than a year later, we watched as Abraham lost his house and other valuables, and was still in debt. My wealthy colleague said to me, "if only he had listened to the whispers of the night and read the writings on the wall, his fate would have been different." The same person who came up to him with a proposition of becoming partners and having lesser costs was responsible for putting him out of business. Abraham couldn't pay his debt, because the yield he expected wasn't forthcoming, his competitors were relentless and invested in improvement, while he was busy spending extravagantly. He sold his oranges before they were ripe and he paid the price. Whatever investment you shall indulge in, you must seek to improve with the overtime. What worked today may not work tomorrow, and that's why I have always clamored for flexibility.

You need to bear in mind the following as you progress, Abraham never had a Good Team around him, because if he had, they would have advised him on the model they operated and was best for business. He was stuck in his ways, and never thought about diversifying. When the storm came, he had no shelter to shield him. His debts were so high, all his assets were taken away, yet he still owed. In the end, he was out of business, giving the public a bad notion about him. His fall from grace didn't start in a day, the signs were there for him to see, but he ignored them all, until he also became ignored, and lost everything in what seemed like a night.

His case is a lesson to you, learn from mistakes to better your investments. This is why knowledge is good, don't stop acquiring them even as you progress. Learn from people's mistakes, experiences and their achievements. It's all a form of acquiring knowledge that's free. Learning from Abraham.

The right people: A potential business partner with brilliant ideas approaches you on cost reduction and business improvement, yet you turn him down and take no action. Then he trades the same products cheaper, yet you conveniently brag about a better brand and higher quality, so consumers will not patronize him, and still do nothing. Profits begin to decline, and panic sets in, shifting blames and pointing fingers, and you still didn't come up with a solution. That was the case of Abraham. All this made it possible for a competition to put him out of business in less than a year. Just imagine he had a team that was good at their jobs, they would have prevented this from happening long ago.

You must make sure you have the right people working for and with you always. Abraham had his friends working for him, and so always wanted to please them. He failed to realize that life is indeed a battlefield, and one must be prepared for the fight all the time. From the greatest to the least in hierarchy, you must ensure they are right for their position. My wealthy college would brag, "I have the best of the best in what they do, and I make sure they don't reduce that standard". It's true that you are the one with the vision, and so you know what you want, but you must be able to have a good team you can delegate to properly handle tasks and they must understand your vision clearly. It all begins with you, because who you are will attract the kind of people around you, ensure that you are an example of what you want and desire to achieve.

Also have in mind that there are no perfect people, so do not expect people to be exactly like you. The aim is to reduce the workload on you, as you progress in your form of investment, ensure you operate a model that will require your constant presence less often. Ensure the satisfaction of these people working for you, make them feel they are a part of something big, and they will go to the ends of the earth for you. Having the right people can be difficult for a start, but it's a thing of joy to make mistakes and learn from them. See these people as an extension of you my child, do not do to them what you wouldn't want done to you, and always make sure you are moral in your dealings with them. Whatever you are willing to achieve must be understood clearly and how they function in making that a reality must also be spelt out or you will be leading a blind flock. The plan is to have the right people to delegate to, the right people that will seek the growth of your investment, and the right people that have the nerve to try new things that will lead to improvement.

When talking about the right people, I mean both people working for you and with you. Your lawyer must be right, your bank and banker must be right, your accountant must be right, your managers must be right, your janitors must be right, your product or service must be right, never compromise standard or cut corners when it comes to utilizing the strength and knowledge of the right people.

Growth and expansion: As you take pain in organizing the right people to function with, overtime you will face growth and the need to expand. Abraham had the visitor of expansion knocking on his door, but he ignored the call. If he had accepted the offer, improved his business model thus maximizing profit, he would have expanded beyond his imagination. But he chose to be in his position and work with his limitations.

When you see constant rise in profitability, and there is a need to expand, do not run away from it, or someone else will do the expansion at your own loss. Many people will fail at this one, because they will be in a hurry to expand without the necessary preparation. You have the right people around you in a team, each functioning in a key role and understanding their duties, with time, there will be need for expansion and bigger roles for them, ensure they are prepared for this or it will be a waste of time, resources and effort.

Once the growth is improving, understand the reason behind the expansion, understand the terrane you are expanding to, understand its relevance to your vision, understand the importance it will offer, think all these through with the right people you have on your side and decide when it's best you expand. Remember, money beget money, that was the simple rule of investment you started with, do not throw it away. Your investment should be able to care for another investment (Even if it's at a minimal level) before you should think of expansion. If you feel the profit will not do such, and after careful analysis you feel borrowing should be an option, ensure at least 50% is funded by your investment, and try as much as possible to repay all debt beforehand. It may be difficult to expand without debt, so outsourced funds should be encouraged only if you are certain it is the right call, and your team is ready for such transition.

Ensure your vision is always understood, and even the area of diversification isn't short of the right people, in other words, make it as valuable as when you started, and work as diligently as you have worked with the right knowledge and people. Never fail to also invest in knowledge as you expand, for it will help in ensuring your stability and relevance, therefore invest in the right form of knowledge to your benefit.

Diversification: As your growth and expansion flourishes, remember the saying "Do not put all your eggs in one basket". You have come a long way my child, and it will be an awful thing when the basket falls and all eggs are broken. You have the right people around you, and have invested in profitable knowledge, always diversify your portfolio. Try something new again, start from the scratch and see it become a giant, seek the right knowledge and resource to ensure it becomes a reality, and even if the basket falls, you'll have another basket full of eggs.

Let the right people who work for and with you handle their bit, while you venture into another form of investment. Think of it as a farm where you started out planting just vegetables, you have grown and expanded, what happens if there is low demand for vegetables or there is high supply? Your profit will be limited. But then again you have another farm where you plant corn, and another where you plant beans, and another for oranges, and another for livestock rearing, and another to package the farm produce, and another involved in the supply chain, and another involved in research and development, that's diversification. The beautiful thing is to put the right people to work while you provide them with the necessary resource and enabling environment to make this a reality.

Is it difficult? Starting off is always the difficult part, but once it becomes reality, the feeling you get cannot be explained with words. Never forget the tools, never forget to always use the right people in areas of their strength. Channel excess funds to where they are needed and make them generate more funds, that's how diversification works. If you feel something will have a significant impact in the future, venture into it with the right people. Do not work yourself up with the feeling that you can do it all my child, let people shine in their own rights, that's how you encourage growth within the system. If you do everything yourself due to unnecessary thirst for perfection or the ultimate, it will result in low productivity. Remember, your job is give the right people what they need to increase productivity. You are like the farmer; you know the right quantity of water, right soil, right amount of fertilizer, and right amount of sunlight a plant needs to grow into a tree and bear fruits, give it to your workers and smile at your harvest.

Insurance: While I was working, I never insured anything that wasn't mandatory to insure. Not just me, but many people too. We saw insurance as a way of taking from us money we may never get back all in the name of security from future uncertainties. But the wealthy people understand the benefits of insurance, and they do not take it for granted.

We had a get together one fine Saturday at a friend's place, and it was going well, until my rich colleague to get a call from one of his executives to watch the local news. Well, we all sat watching the news with sympathy for him, three houses in one of his estates were on fire and it was spreading. Suddenly he turned off the TV and said, "This news will only spoil our mood, it's a fine Saturday, lets enjoy it without limitations" then he started sipping on his drink and encouraging small talks. Many of us weren't the same after watching that, we felt a chill within us, even if it wasn't ours, because we knew it was his, we felt sympathy. But he on the other hand, after watching that was as cheerful as he was before watching it, and it only made us more surprised. Maybe it made us pity him more, since we were sure when he goes home he will moan as expected. However, we were wrong; he came to work that Monday and acted normal. I couldn't understand his coolness to the event that happened that Saturday, that I walked up to him during lunch (Everyone ate at the same cafeteria) and asked how he managed to keep his cool regardless of the event that occurred. My wealthy colleague laughed and said, "The only thing I lost is a couple of weeks for them to investigate, but insurance will take care of everything, that's what I pay them for."

Dear child, remember when I stated that you should have the right people around you, never disregard the right insurance policy for your investment and do not default in payment.

Diversification is a form of insurance too, but take advantage of insurance companies that will favor you. Insure everything that needs to be insured, from staff to assets, ensure you do not joke with this. It may look like an unnecessary cost, but what happens when there is a fire or an accident resulting to loss of life? Life is full of uncertainties, and you should ensure that you employ the right people to determine the right insurance policy so when the storm comes, you will have shelter.

Tax, Government Regulation and Liability: Yet again the right people is an advantage when dealing with areas of tax, liability or government regulation. Wherever you choose to operate, there are laws of that land that affect you. It may come in form of tax or government regulations, please never take them for granted. In my time, I have seen mighty corporations fall just because they evaded tax or due to an unfavorable government regulations or liabilities. For tax, ensure you have the right people that will ensure you benefit from tax avoidance as often as possible, it is not a crime. However, never in any circumstance evade tax, that is a big crime, and you my child are no criminal. As for government policies, try to stay as relevant as possible so the government sees your benefit and policies are in your favor, pay up every levy or tariff due to the government, compounding them may leave you without smiles. Network with the right people in government so you can stay updated and act fast to protect your interest and that of the people that work with or for you beforehand. As for liabilities, know when your investment is heading for the rocks, study the trends and jump boat before the ship sinks, or ensure you have the right people jump into the water and mend the leakage if the need be. Do not owe debts you cannot repay, as a matter of fact, avoid debts as much as you can and only seek them if need be.

It all boils down to the right people, have them work for you and you won't have a problem unlike when you act like a jack of all trade. People have strengths and weaknesses, play on that strength and make your investment better. Give to the government what is required after the necessary tax avoidance, pay all levies and dues as required, and avoid compounding debt, ensure they are serviced as at when due. If you feel your investment is losing ground, do not be skeptical in pulling out and seeking another venture to invest in. In all, have the right network of people that will feed you information, even about your very competitors, ensure you are aware of the times and be flexible in your dealings with the situations. Never in any case allow your investment be a part of a scandal that will lead to public outcry. From bribery to amoral practices to forced labor, ensure it is avoided like a plague or pull out from such investment if it require indulging in such acts, for eventually the world will know the truth, and you may be unable to stomach the after effect of such practices.

Public Relations: My child, another thing many people fail to understand is the power of public relations, never underestimate it. Always ensure whatever investment you make has a positive public relation, from consumers to competitors to suppliers, to employees, to the government. It can be achieved by ensuring compliance with the necessary laws or rules and regulation, ensuring the right people that work for and with you are well compensated, focusing on problems and proffering simple solutions rather that complicate issues and many more.

In this period of your life, do not be afraid to take risk. Never entertain greed, never disregard people, trust no one yet act like you trust everyone, no one is irreplaceable so don't get too emotionally involved. As you increase your investment portfolio, never fail to also increase your assets. However, I'll still maintain you refrain from reckless spending and friends whose major motive is to have fun, you at this stage should be wise enough to know when to merry and when to work. I commend you for attaining this stage of your life when it finally happens, and I know you already know the importance of money, the right people and time. When it' all said and done, there will be time for rest, so toil all you can today, so that your rest will be long and peaceful.

Chapter Four

Early Retirement Phase

I was at a conference in Berlin long ago and got acquainted with a guy in his mid-thirties, he was an investor and I was amazed at how far he has come in such a short time. I was more amazed when he said he was going to Dubai the following day to relax, and then Paris to check out some high valued artifact. "Are you on leave or something?" I asked. He simply replied by saying, "I'm retired, so I'm always on leave?" We both laughed, but he was dead serious. He understood the system of obtaining wealth and he followed it through, and before he was thirty-seven, he was retired.

Many employees wake up in the morning and go to their place of work not because they want to, but because they need to. They need to protect their pension, they need to protect their salary, they need to protect their bonuses, because if they don't, they will be facing a disastrous month ahead. Therefore, the cycle continues and they believe they are working to safeguard their future. Once they attain the retirement age, they seem fulfilled relying on pension and whatever minimal savings they have managed to save up. They go on fancy vacations that get boring because their kids are somewhere working or in college. They are probably divorced because they made work more of a priority and neglected their marriage, in all, they feel lonely. They enjoy the luxury of time at an old age, some are lucky not to get bored or feel unfulfilled, but a large majority feel like they have not lived after a period and crave to have their jobs back.

You on the other hand should endeavor to attain that luxury before the age of thirty-five, and even at an old age, you will be glad because you have lived. The early retirement period is when you must ensure all your investments and assets are capable of seeing you and your family through without you visiting those investments. The measure of wealth is simply the number of years you can spend without seeking additional income, and in many wealthy people's case, that's generations.

Know value and assets; acquire them as often as you can. From tuition to trust fund to vacations, plan ahead for your family's needs, plan everything. Before you are forty, you will have enough time to spend with your family and friends.

Ants understand this principle to an extent, and we can learn from them and improve it. During a fine weather, they work hard and store as much as possible, and await the period when the weather changes. When the weather changes, they are safe within their comfort zone enjoying what they have amassed. Like you my child, invest in so much when there is plenty and buy different assets.

Let more skilled people handle the day to day activities, while you channel excess funds to where they are required by investing in more diversified portfolio. Before forty, those investments must finance as many assets as you want to acquire and all expenses, while you have enough time to relax, and coordinate in your preferred method.

You have your family time, you have your fun time, you have your personal time, that's the goal. Not every day will belong to work, but you will be able to know when your presence is required and when it's not, because you have the right kind of people working for you. Your ears and eyes in this period should scout for the best deals, especially those in relation to your assets. Assets bring in money for you, even when you are not there, so be careful on what you will term as an asset.

If you want a vacation, asset A should be able to take care of the cost. If your wife wants to change her wardrobe, she has asset B to thank for it. You have a family function that requires donation; asset C will fix that. Your child wants to school at Harvard; asset D handles it without much ado. That's how you retire early my child, once you can increase your investment portfolio and also your asset arsenal, you will be on leave every day.

Chapter Five

On Love and Family

On Love: I will begin by quoting a poem from one of my favorite poets – **Don-Kels DaDevin** – titled **Dream Flower**:

> *"In a garden of gorgeous flowers;*
> *Blooming without gloom – the colour of all flowers*
> *But in my quest for the most valuable*
> *I ferret the same thicket and hook over and over*
> *My search for an illuminating ornamental petal*
> *Lead to the finding of a splendid rainbow tinted flower*
> *With flourishing carpel, beaming for every to behold*
> *A pride to the Gardener this dream flower stands out*
> *Yet more pride to the beholder*
> *Admired by every lily and rose*
> *This dream flower possesses zealous qualities*
> *That the beholder cannot withstand but adore*
> *Thanks be the Gardener for the flourishing qualities of this dream flower – You"*

My child, there is time to seek love, time to seek wealth, and it's usually a problem when you seek both at the wrong time. I have advised you not to indulge in profitless relationships with women, but a time will come when one woman will stand out in your life, and she shall be like the dream flower the poet described. Everyone finds love differently, so I cannot say when it's best to find love, but in your pursuit for wealth, love shouldn't be a top priority. However, if you find that special someone that will compliment you even if you are yet to get wealth, never fail to make your feeling known and ensure you seek stability between your relationship and goals. You will be heartbroken a couple of times, if you are lucky you will not, but in all do not fail to try again. Do not give your all, until you are certain she is right, then talk to her about your dreams and aspiration. A good lady will see your greatness and support you through thick and thin, but a good lady is hard to find.

Never be in a rush to find love, you will find it eventually. The beginning is what determines a lot, if you fall in love with a lady for her beauty, she will get old and you will seek another. If it's the pleasure you derive from your union, it will get boring and you will seek something more pleasurable. Looks or pleasure shouldn't be your driving force in seeking love, however it will be a fortune if love possesses both. Above all, love must be compatible, love must be you friend, love must be your best friend, love must be your lover, love must be your fortified arena, love must be your strength and weakness, love must stand the test of time, love must bring you happiness, love must respect you for who you are and not want to change you, love must make you want to be a better you, love must add value to your existence, love must be the spice to your life, love must be understanding, love must be ready to stand with you at all times, love must be the best thing you have ever had, love must be that dream flower you seek, it must be the most valuable.

No one is perfect, always remember that. If love meets as many of these criteria as possible, never fail to be the love of that person's life by being the best you can and fulfilling the above requirements. There will be times when things won't be as electrifying as they were in the beginning, but you must remember to always strive to make good memories that will keep the fire burning regardless of the time. When you both know it's right and decide to spend the rest of your lives together, do not hesitate in making that *Dream Flower* your wife.

Wife: Yet again I'll quote the poet ***Don-Kels DaDevin*** poem ***Forever:***

> *"That our days be honey sweet*
> *And nights as the seaside peace*
> *I have toiled beyond thy waters*
> *And tasted from sweeter vines*
> *My eyes having beheld many beauties*
> *Still my heart never forgoes thee*
> *And this eyes long to see thee over*
> *No fruit ripens my lips as thine*
> *No wine compares to those from your hips*
> *As I go on and on in life*
> *Sweet or foul words cannot push you yonder*
> *Thus forever in my heart*
> *Forever in this heart of mine you shall bloom"*

Since you have found a good lady and made her your wife, you should know that it's a lifetime affair. In my time, I have seen many start off as lovebirds, and then in years to come they employ the services of divorce lawyers. I tell you my child, divorce should never be an option for you because it's more expensive and emotionally destabilizing than you would expect, that is why you must choose carefully when finding a wife. Many will advise you to sign a prenuptial agreement so there won't be future worries, well you can go ahead and follow that road, but have it in mind that divorce should never be an option between you.

When issues arise, solve it as a couple; do not make your problems public. Make sure you listen to each other and strive to always seek solutions to your differences rather than point fingers and raise dust. She is your wife, both of you are one, so never take her for granted but respect her. Seek her advice and counsel at all times, because she might have more to add and save you from yourself. Be a good husband, do not let work take away moments you should have shared together and make good memories. Love conquers all, so never stop showing love. No matter how old you are, always look into her eyes with admiration and tell her how beautiful she is and how blessed you are to have her as your queen. Yes, she is your queen, and you are her king, always treat her like the queen she is by giving her full attention and time. She will be the mother of your kids, do not provoke her by having worthless affairs that will eventually break your home. Adorn her with whatever pleases you so your eyes are fixed on her only. You are a team, never forget that.

You both must learn to constantly feed your intimacy as often as possible, so external persona don't interfere and cause more damage in the future than good. Forgiveness is crucial, learn to say "I'm sorry" and "Thank you" and forgive when your partner is seeking for it.

Children: I may not have been a good father to you, do not make the mistake of not being a good father to your children. You must give them the space they require, yet you must be close to them. They should be able to tell you their fears and their aspirations, and ensure you strive to be the best. All they would want is for you to understand them, therefore be an understanding father, never to teach them what I have taught you and ensure they are discipline. Your children are an image of you, they learn from you and your wife, always act moral so they do not see a reason to be rebellious. Never deprive them of what the need to be the best, still never spoil them.

You might be wealthy, but they must find their own path, do not force them into your path. Every child shall be unique, encourage them to be the best in whatever they do. Teach them the values you have learnt with age, and ensure they understand that they are privileged and shouldn't see themselves as better off than others who are deprived. The nurture you give them determines a lot in their dealing with the real world; teach them with practical examples and not just theories.

When they achieve something even little, praise them, show them you are watching and you feel they did well. Never forget their birthdays, important functions, and ceremonies. Know what they need and want, honor them with your presence and the right gifts that wouldn't spoil them. Ensure they understand the concept of money, savings, right people, wealth and independence. Teach them to be good, and all men are equal so they do not grow up being extremist or racist, but morally upright.

In all, take care of them and let them know you care for them. When they come of age, do not be scared to let them go, because you have taught them the principles of life, and everyone has the right to choose. When you are old, it will be their turn to shower you with love, and this will come naturally.

Family: You first priority is your family, never take it for granted. As you progress, ensure you plan for everything with your darling wife. From the kids trust funds, to their college tuition, to health insurance, to family vacation, to monthly feeding and allowances, to anniversary dinners and presents, to birthday celebration and gifts and so much more. Your family is your top priority, and so you must have time for it. There must be a balanced relationship between you, your wife and your kids, they are more of a priority to any extended family, always make sure it is clearly stated.

No matter how busy you may be, never miss dinner more than twice in a week. Ensure there is family time and everyone bonds and talk to each other about issues. Do not default family vacation and ensure there are no distractions during that period, not even work. Respect and forgiveness should be understood by everyone in the family, and practiced. Also, learn to listen and seek everyone's candid opinion before making a decision that will affect any member of the family. You are a team, learn to work as a team. No external person or issue should ever come between you and your family; it is what matters to you most and must be valued.

You might say I know nothing about family and the strength of a family bond, but I want you to learn from my mistakes and from the mistakes of everyone around you and do better. Do not let little issues break the family bond, do not let separation or divorce take a place in your family, believe me, it's ugly. Love your wife unconditionally and respect her, love your children beyond measure and train them in morals, etiquette, standard, equality and equity, and never fail to be a good father, husband, lover, friend, best friend, hero, advocate and mentor to them at all times. Be patient with them and never take them for granted or compare them with others, for they are the best in their own rights, always remind them of how special and unique they are.

Chapter Six

Health

This is one aspect many don't take seriously until they are sick, or a close relative of theirs becomes ill. My child, shunning accidents and disasters, the best way to live long and enjoy your old age is simple by living right from the days of your youth until your death. In your youth, your system is still very active, so can stand a lot of toxicity, but as you grow older, it weakens. Many people fail to realize that and still carry on with their youthful habits to their forties and fifties, and then live a complicated life and scream for the cheaper health care system.

The seed you sow will one day become a tree, so you must remain constantly conscious on what you really sow into your life. Health is wealth, I have seen people lose so much of their fortune to health issues because they didn't live right. However, some health issues are hereditary and cannot be prevented but managed. Ignorance in this regard is deadly, so ensure you are aware and in control of your health situations.

Exercise as often as you can, regardless of your age, exercise is important. A simple hike or a jog done constantly yields more positivity than sleeping and constant relaxing (lazing around). Not just you alone, but your family and loved ones must be taught to exercise frequently.

What you eat and drink is another crucial aspect of a healthy life. Avoid eating late, avoid constant intake of organic food, eat lots of vegetables and fresh food, avoid regular fast-food order, drink plenty water, avoid food high in cholesterol, constantly check your sugar level and blood pressure, and many healthier tips, keep to them.

Ensure you have constant checkup and have doctors as friends. Once there is a change in your body system, seek medical advice from your doctor. Never should you self-medicate or abuse your drugs, let the expert do their job. As for habits, resist addiction as much as you can. From alcohol, to tobacco, to drugs, to energy drinks or enhancement, reduce them to the barest minimum as you grow older, or stay away from them completely. In addition, ensure you give your body the required rest daily.

If you stick to these simple advice, you will enjoy the benefit of good health, even at an old age. Living healthy is cheaper than trying to seek cure from the effects of not eating healthy, always have that in mind. Live healthy, ensure your family lives healthy, and you will enjoy the benefits of having a healthy body.

Chapter Seven

Maintaining Wealth

If you have followed accordingly what I have stated, then getting wealth and maintaining it wouldn't be difficult. You already know what is required, it is left to you to keep doing the right thing and never give up. A time will come when you will feel depressed, but you must remember that to extract juice from an orange, you must squeeze. Therefore, whenever you are depressed, it should do nothing but bring out the best in you.

Maintain a healthy relationship with your friends and family, they are an important part of your life, because they only can show you love or hate directly, and it will either affect or make you emotionally strong. Understand that you shouldn't mix business with pleasure, and so you know when to draw a line.

As for your investments, never forget what made it a reality, those little sacrifices, those people that contributed to your success, those principles that made you discipline, do not take them for granted in the time of plenty. Teach your children the way that I have taught you, and add more from your experience and knowledge.

Always be around the right people and those that make you happy, because happiness is pleasurable than wealth. Pay your taxes, ensure your employees are happy, do not indulge in activities or investments that are shady, don't stop networking, and understand it's not a do or die affair, human lives are more important.

Also to maintain wealth, do not fail to constantly equip yourself with knowledge. Times change, and policies change, you should be wise enough at this stage to know what's best for you and your investments, and take the necessary risks. Work on your weakness and build your strength, people are also watching you, ensure you are always ready.

When the wind of change comes, do not be adamant, change with the times. Upgrade when you should upgrade, let go when necessary, no hard feelings. Opportunities will come, constantly take advantage of them when they present themselves, no matter how little. The early bird catches the worm; ensure your team seeks innovation as early as possible so you benefit from being an early bird.

Chapter Eight

Legacy

After all is said and done, where then is your footprint on earth? What will you be remembered for? What difference did your existence bring to life? What legacy do you leave behind? Dear child, these are questions I want you to ask yourself as you steadily rise to the top.

I'll make this as simple as I can, give back to the public. There is a philosophy of Ubuntu that simple means - I am who I am because of you. No man made it great alone, and as you walk the path of wealth and greatness, how positively do you want to affect others around you so they also walk their own path?

You have resources at your disposal, do not be selfish with it. Humanity's problems are many, so focus your attention and resources in bringing good change in a particular area that will win your heart. Nothing good is too little, ensure you save as many people as possible from a sinking ship, that way you have added additional value to the society.

When leaving a legacy, ensure you do not do it for the glory, do it to really affect lives positively. People need help, help as much as you can for the sake of helping. The little seeds you plant should make substantial difference to humanity when they become trees, so even when you are gone, you will be appreciated for the little effort you put in that made a difference.

Wealth is not gotten over night, therefore ensure your children understands the principles and follow them through. Plan all the way to the very end, so even your successor is known if the need be before you depart the earth. Above all, never underestimate the power of love. Show love as often as you can, people need it in their lives.

Dear child, I'm glad you have come this far, there is one thing to know, there is another thing to act, therefore act right. Be flexible with all I have stated, the journey will be long, but always keep your eyes on the prize. I know it won't be easy as I have stated, but do not give up, seek strength and believe in who you are. People have made wealth from nothing, during my time it happened so frequently, and I know yours will not be any different. Be part of those that will leave their mark on earth for the good they have done, don't just come and leave without a purpose.

The road to the top of the mountain is long and bumpy, but with determination it is not impossible. The storm will come, the sun will shine, but in the end, all that must be in your mind is getting to the mountain peak. Once you have gotten there, help as many people as you can to also get to the mountain peak, for there is room for everyone.

When all is said and done, remember to leave a lasting legacy behind that generations will hear of and be glad you walked the surface of the earth. Not just as a wealthy man, but as a great man. This is my guide to you my child, it's left to you to follow or neglect the ways, choose wisely.

CONTACT

E.I. Kelvin

Email

kelsdadadevin@gmail.com

Social Media

Twitter.com/Don_Kels

www.ingramcontent.com/pod-product-compliance
Lightning Source LLC
Chambersburg PA
CBHW021437170526
45164CB00001B/284